GW01017670

SUMMARY
OF
On Tyranny:

Twenty Lessons from the Twentieth
Century

By

Timothy Snyder

PrintRight

PrintRight

Copyright (c) 2020

Table of Content

SYNOPSIS:

On Tyranny (2017) is a guide to recognizing the warning signs of tyranny, which, unfortunately, is a political climate that many are all too familiar with. Find out what you can do to protect yourself and keep your community vigilant and resistant to dangerous political leaders.

ABOUT THE AUTHOR:

Timothy Snyder is a Professor of History at Yale University. His other books include Bloodlands: Europe Between Hitler and Stalin and Black Earth: The Holocaust as History and Warning.

DISCLAIMER:

This book is a SUMMARY. It is meant to be a companion, not a replacement, to the original book. Please note that this summary is not authorized, licensed, approved, or endorsed by the author or publisher of the main book. The author of this summary is wholly responsible for the content of this summary and is not associated with the original author or publisher of the main book. If you'd like to purchase the original book, kindly search for the title in the search box.

INTRODUCTION.

What's in it for me? Get the historic insights needed to identify and resist tyranny.

Until recently, many Americans believed that the future would bring, however gradually, progress – that we would continue inching toward a globalized world of prosperity and reason. The twentieth century's history of Fascism, Nazism and Communism seemed like a grim, distant past that could never return.

However, in the coming years, things may very well change. It seems that tyranny may once again be on the horizon. So what can we do?

Luckily for us, history can teach us how to recognize and resist tyranny. These blinks, based on the polemical ideas of historian Timothy Snyder, will shed some light on what we can learn from the past about tyranny.

You'll also find out

- how to avoid going along with a tyrannical regime's agenda;
- why reading books is a great way to resist tyranny; and
- how to protect truth from death.

RESIST TYRANNY BY BEING POLITICALLY ACTIVE AND AWARE OF PARAMILITARY FORCES.

If you've been following the news these days, you'll no doubt know that America is bristling with hostile attitudes toward "foreign threats." However, if you have a real concern about threats to democracy, it's often best to keep an eye on the threats from within.

If you look at the democratic governments that have collapsed in the years since World War I, you'll notice that each fell to a single party that seized power from within the nation.

Nazis, communists and fascists have traditionally used spectacle and repression to enable their takeovers. They've also tended to use salami tactics, the process of slicing away at the opposition, taking power piece by piece. Often the public is too distracted to notice the threat to their freedom.

This is why you must be vigilant and support a multiparty system. What you want to avoid is one power controlling every level of the government, which is what is now happening in the United States.

You can do your part by voting, in both local and state elections, and being politically active. It's best to support the use of paper ballots, which can't be tampered with as easily as electronic ones. And of course, you could even run for local office yourself.

In the meantime, another sign to beware of is paramilitary forces – that is, any military presence that isn't state or federally sanctioned.

If someone wants to take over, she'll likely throw together some sort of violent organization that acts as a paramilitary wing of her political party.

Donald Trump did something that most candidates avoid; he formed a private security force that followed his orders at political rallies. They were used to eject dissenting voices from the rallies, and the members even encouraged supporters to remove anyone who opposed the candidate.

At one rally, Trump gave a disturbing command: "Get the remnant out!" After "the remnant" had been removed, he asked the crowd, "Isn't this more fun than a regular boring rally? To me, it's fun."

This is the kind of behavior that should make people take notice.

DON'T IGNORE DANGEROUS LANGUAGE AND SYMBOLISM; TAKE A STAND AGAINST IT.

When the Nazi Party came to power in Germany, one of their first acts was to call for a boycott of all Jewish businesses. At first, this call was met with indifference from the population. But then storefronts began to be painted with the words "Jewish" or "Aryan" – and, before long, the racism was gaining traction.

The language and symbolism a political party uses may initially seem meaningless, or even ridiculous, but these simple tools can lead to profound consequences.

The marking of storefronts in Germany wasn't just racism; it also exploited people's greed and survival instincts.

Other business owners and hopeful entrepreneurs knew that if a shop was marked "Jewish" it would soon be out of business. This meant competition would be reduced, and prime commercial real estate would soon be available. All of these things played into the desires of a public that was looking for ways out of their own economic hardships.

Even if the signs of tyranny seem harmless or temporary, it's important to take them seriously and not allow them to fester and grow.

The blame can't be placed solely on those who painted the storefronts; the ones who remained passive and accepted these actions as a normal change in society were also complicit in the murders that soon followed.

Therefore, to avoid giving imagery tyrannical power, you should refuse to display any symbols that represent a party that excludes anyone.

In 1978, the political dissident and future Czechoslovakian president, Vaclav Havel, wrote The Power of the Powerless, an essay about a grocer who put a simple sign in his storefront window. The sign was for the Communist Party, and it read, "Workers of the world, unite!"

While the man didn't support the party, he put up the sign to avoid trouble with the authorities. But as the essay makes clear, such submissiveness is still harmful.

By accepting the regime's games as the new norm, or by choosing the path of least resistance, you're still playing into its hands and enabling the game to go on.

The only way to prevent the regime from continuing to persecute its "enemies" is to refuse to play along.

AVOID FALLING VICTIM TO PROPAGANDA BY READING AND STAYING INFORMED.

Even if you don't follow politics, it can be hard to ignore the slogans and sound bites that politicians will repeat ad nauseam in the media.

You can avoid getting caught up in the buzzwords and clichéd thinking by being an individual and seeking out and expressing your own ideas.

George Orwell's book 1984 is about a populace that is being starved of creativity and independent thinking by an all-powerful media that employs suffocatingly constrictive language. Over time, the ruling party has eliminated more and more words from the official dictionary in order to weaken people's minds and their ability to resist the ideas of the regime. This way, they'll come to accept the party's contradictory slogan: "War is peace; freedom is slavery; ignorance is strength."

There is a lot of truth to Orwell's premise that we need to use the words we have to fight tyranny and keep independent thought alive. It's when we resort to programmed thinking, and repeating the slogans and clichés of politicians, that we lose the ability to learn from the past, understand the present and see what the future has in store.

One of the best ways to think clearly for yourself is to read books and cut yourself off from the media and the internet.

If avoiding the internet is an unrealistic proposition, the least you can do is broaden your sources of information. If you only read or listen to one source, or rely wholly on the mainstream media, you're bound to end up repeating the same sound bites and prepackaged information that politicians want you to hear.

But books are the best way to get informed and think for yourself, as they offer context and reveal the gray areas between good and bad. They also offer insight into how other people live, all of which is useful information to have these days.

Even popular novels like Harry Potter can provide great messages to live by. You may have missed it as a child, but much of the conflict in the Harry Potter universe concerns a resistance to tyranny.

BREAK DOWN SOCIAL BARRIERS TO KEEP YOUR COMMUNITY ALIVE AND HEALTHY.

Consider this question: What does making eye contact have to do with politics?

The answer is connectedness. Too often, we walk around looking at our devices and not at one another. To make eye contact isn't about being polite; it's about being a responsible citizen who is a connected part of the community.

Tyranny succeeds when it separates communities by erecting social barriers that isolate and distract people. But resistance can succeed by breaking these barriers down and bringing people from different backgrounds together to exchange ideas about how they can move forward together.

Therefore, resistance to tyranny starts when different social circles come together.

In Poland, a successful resistance to Communism was possible after the Solidarity labor movement built a coalition of diverse people. By banding together, Catholic workers and professionals from the secular community were able to win seats in the Polish government.

In 1968, the Communist regime had turned workers against students who were protesting for change. And in Gdansk, in 1970, striking workers were met with violent suppression.

It took the coming together of intellectuals and workers, in 1976, to finally change the government. These people were not united by religion or political orientation; rather, they bonded over common goals.

The alliance grew stronger in 1980, when Polish workers in Gdansk came out on strike again. But this time they had lawyers, students and other workers to tip the scales in their favor. A free labor union soon followed, and the Solidarity movement became 10 million strong.

It lasted 16 months. The Communist regime in Poland finally declared martial law to crush the movement. Ironically, in 1989, with the regime in turmoil, the Communists were forced to seek help from Solidarity leaders, who won free elections in return for their alliance.

It marked the beginning of the end for Communism in Poland, and eastern Europe and the Soviet Union soon followed.

FREEDOM DEPENDS ON CONTROLLING YOUR INFORMATION, SO PROTECT YOUR PRIVACY.

You might feel comfortable sharing certain details on Facebook, but it's important to realize to what extent your personal freedom goes hand in hand with the access others have to your personal information.

Think about it. The less control you have over who can read your personal details and correspondence, the more personal freedom you're giving up.

It hardly matters whether it's Google, the US government or Russian intelligence agencies that are accessing the information. You need to protect what's yours or else it'll no longer be considered private – and soon other rights you thought were inherent will also be taken away.

We now know that hacking into private correspondence can humiliate and cause major disruption.

In the 2016 US election, stolen emails from the Democratic National Committee and members of the Clinton campaign threw the election into chaos and moved the nation a step closer to totalitarianism.

For the most part, the media just made matters worse by simply treating this violation of privacy like any other news item, which only served to distract voters from what was actually happening.

The media are prone to exploiting our natural interest in gossip about others. Hannah Arendt, one of the twentieth century's foremost philosophers, understood the human appetite for secrets – as well as its dangers.

Arendt noticed that people often find conspiracy theories more attractive than the humdrum facts and reality of politics. We're easily seduced by the prospect of dark secrets and scandalous revelations. The problem is that our interest in these often erroneous theories distracts us from other, more concrete political issues.

Sure, pretty much everyone constantly checks phones for media updates and blithely shares their personal information, but this doesn't mean you should. In fact, when everyone engages in the same activity, it's a warning sign that society is falling victim to the irrational mob.

So protect your freedom by securing your privacy.

Cut back on using the internet and, when you can, talk face-to-face instead of using third-party software. And ask yourself, when's the last time I checked for malware?

Tyrannical regimes will use any means to make the populace fearful, so don't give them ammunition by leaving your personal information up for grabs.

BE ON THE LOOKOUT FOR THE DIFFERENT WAYS IN WHICH TYRANNICAL LEADERS DISTORT THE TRUTH.

Today has been called the "post-truth" era, a time when facts are repeatedly dismissed in favor of alternative ones. It might seem absurd, but it's a very real threat, for after truth dies, freedom is usually next.

There are four stages in the process of truth getting so twisted that it no longer exists, the first of which is open hostility to verifiable truth and reality.

During this stage, lies are presented as facts, which is something President Trump does remarkably often. One study showed that 78 percent of his claims during the 2016 campaign were false.

The second stage is marked by an endless repetition of the same lies, the idea being that if you say something often enough, people will start to believe it.

On Twitter and in speeches, phrases like "Crooked Hillary" and "Lock her up!" show up again and again. Even though the truth is readily available, the repetition tries to rewrite it.

In the third stage, contradictions are openly embraced.

Trump promised tax cuts and the elimination of the national debt and an increase in spending on defense programs. Clearly, these promises directly contradict one another. To think that the person making them wasn't aware of these contradictions would be to abandon all reason.

The fourth stage is characterized by misplaced faith in leaders who pronounce themselves as the "voice of the people" or the savior of a nation's true values. Such a voice, such a savior, has never existed. So to believe such propaganda doesn't only put truth at risk; it also chips away at our freedom.

This is the same language that preceded the fascist movement of the 1930s, and the great Romanian playwright Eugène Ionesco saw many of his friends fall under its spell. Such enchantment became the basis of his absurdist play Rhinoceros, in which people who accepted the propaganda as truth transformed into a certain horned animal.

If you asked people for their opinion when the Nazi party was just starting, most would say they were against it. Yet, one by one, over a series of years, most of them accepted it. In the end, the resistance was quite small. But history doesn't have to repeat itself.

FINAL SUMMARY

The key message in this book:

Protecting your country from tyranny is a matter of knowing what to look for. The telltale signs include the slow erosion of personal freedoms, threats to your privacy and a disregard for facts and truth. Unfortunately, these signs are all too apparent in the United States today. We must be vigorous in defending facts, reason and respect for human dignity.

Actionable advice:

Don't engage in defeatist thinking, and read up on the origins of totalitarianism.

A lot of people think, "I'm not powerful enough to change anything, so why should I bother participating in politics?" It's an understandable sentiment, but it's also a very flawed one, and one that fails to grasp how change really occurs.

Change doesn't happen all at once, in some grand fashion – it happens slowly, whether it's for the better or the worse. So remember: every little bit helps and don't let yourself get into the self-fulfilling cycle of defeatist thinking.